Jett's Job

The true adventures of a traveling petting farm

By

Beth T. Stambaugh

authorHOUSE™

1663 LIBERTY DRIVE, SUITE 200
BLOOMINGTON, INDIANA 47403
(800) 839-8640
WWW.AUTHORHOUSE.COM

First published by AuthorHouse 12/28/05

ISBN: 1-4259-0749-0 (sc)

Printed in the United States of America
Bloomington, Indiana

This book is printed on acid-free paper.

Dedicated...

…to all my petting farm help-words can not express my gratitude

…to all my riding students, past and present, you have all taught me

…to all my close friends, your help and understanding will live with me forever

…to my husband, Jerry, your devotion, patience, and love motivates me daily

…to my two children, Toni and Ian, you both inspire me. I love you.

…to Bub and Meg for Jett

…to Jett – who not only helped me make a living but helped me make a life.

Table of Contents

Two Boys 1

The Cast 15

Solo Appearances..............................29

On the Road 41

Our Home..53

The Fair...63

Two Boys

I just stood there like I always do. It is my job to just stand there nice and quiet, trying not to worry about the things going on around me. It can get boring sometimes but it is a lot less exhausting than my previous job. Occasionally I shift my weight from one leg to the other because I get tired. All I have to do is just stand there. I have food in front of me all the time so I eat all day and when I am thirsty someone brings me all the water I could possibly drink.

This really is a great job, it is also very entertaining. The people who come and just stare are quite amusing. Like the two boys who just stood there staring and whispering. I had to really strain to hear what they were saying, because of my age I think my hearing is dwindling. After awhile I finally heard them and I couldn't believe what they said "What do you think it is and do you think he is real or is he stuffed?"

What in the world are they thinking? I realize I am in the city because of all the concrete but haven't these young men ever seen a horse tied to a trailer before? It's not like it's hard to figure out-four legs, mane and tail- well mine is short but big deal. I am quite a handsome example of the equine world. I stand at a respectable 15.2 hands (4 inches to a hand) and am a very stylish grey roan Appaloosa. Another hint that I am a real, live horse is the fact that I am standing here tied to a HORSE TRAILER not to mention the fact I am tied beside a donkey and we are part of a petting farm! Where is Beth when I need her? She needs to straighten these boys out and educate them to the fact that I am not only alive and well, but I am the backbone of this whole petting farm.

I consider Beth my bodyguard in situations like this because she is always watching over me and all the animals with me. Not only is it her job to ensure that we all have plenty of hay and water and clean up our manure(boy does she ever get all kinds of reactions and comments regarding that work), but she makes sure no one pets us rough, walks where they shouldn't or do anything ridiculous that non-animal people would do.

Beth generally has lots of help. Most of her help consists of her riding students, past and present. She is a horseback riding instructor and also trains horses. Her success is greatly due to the fact that I was her primary school horse and before that her partner in the competitive horse world. Her students are more than an asset to her and her petting farm business. They are all very close friends and all her students have been an inspiration to her. However, if it hadn't been for my excellent teaching talents as a horse, none of them would be the humans they are today. Fortunately, in this petting farm adventure, they think highly of me also and act as other bodyguards.

The whole petting farm thing all started as a joke or a sarcastic comment from Beth's husband. He presented her with a donkey one year for Christmas and made the comment "Well how is she going to earn her keep here on the farm?" Beth knew the importance of every animal on the farm having a purpose. This also seemed as good of an excuse as any to get more animals on the farm. Some how she came up with the idea of a petting farm. Making it a traveling petting farm would mean no more traffic into the already busy horse farm. The idea of calling it a petting farm and not a zoo was simple- only have domestic animals, nothing exotic. This idea escalated into a full scale family business, involving her husband, two children, and her longest family member- me!

So as I stand here tied to our gooseneck horse trailer, beside my very good friend Molly, the donkey, I listen in disbelief to the two young boys. There is nothing I can do but stand still and maybe try to snooze a bit amongst all the noise in this concrete building.

"I don't think he is alive. Maybe he is stuffed or something." The two boys are still standing whispering to each other. I am listening to this nonsense when I hear Beth's voice, "Of course he is alive! His name is Jett. He has been with me for about 22 years."

"He's your horse?" they ask her.

"Sure is. So are all these animals."

"You own all these animals?" They ask her. These two boys sure looked like city kids-clean shoes and a definite look of fear combined with curiosity.

"Sure do," she replied, sounding like the teacher she is.

"How do you get them all here? Do they all fit in that trailer?" one boy asks pointing to the horse trailer, while the other boy asked the most popular question, "What do you live on a farm or something?" Their curiosity is truly peaked at this point.

Right, kid, we all live in a development, or better yet, an apartment in the city, I think to myself. Beth has more patience with these people than I do. Now let's think about this question, kid. This particular petting farm consists of me-the handsome, extremely talented (at least in my prime) Appaloosa horse and my very beautiful partner, (despite her large ears), Molly, the Donkey, tied to the trailer. All of the other animals are split between two chain link kennels that are attached to each other and then somehow hooked behind Molly and myself. I think that is some sort of barricade to keep people from walking behind us. All of this is then attached to the truck and trailer. In one of the chain link kennels is a pot-bellied pig named Julie. Julie has to share her kennel with two pygmy goats named Judy and Jerry. In the other kennel is a calf named Tyler and a blind sheep named Lilly. Continuing our tour around there are smaller individual kennels. One kennel with a rabbit named Gene, another has ducks that were hatched out of an incubator, and another houses a rooster named Red and a hen named Betty. As if that is not enough, there is a large kennel with a very large and loud goose named Andy Goose. Last, but certainly not least, is a Bassett hound named Butter. Sure kid, looking at all these animals I think an educated guess would be that we all live on a farm.

"Yes they all live on my farm with my family and me."

"What, you got kids too?" the boy asked her. No kid she lives in the barn with all us animals. The questions just keep coming and never cease to amaze me, being the worldly horse that I am.

Beth points to a little blond girl that is holding a baby duck for people to pet. "Just use one finger to pet the duck," the girl says to the crowd of kids and adults around her. "That's my daughter and my son is the boy who is holding the rabbit for people to pet. Would you both like to pet Jett and Molly or my son will help you pet the rabbit?"

This brings a panicked reaction from both boys "Are you serious? That big horse might bite my hand off!"

Right again, kid. They bring me and all of these animals here to this festival not so people can experience some farm animals, but to be attacked viciously by a horse, or better yet by a blind sheep. Watch out kid, because as you try to pet me, I'm going to bite your hand off!

"Oh come on, I'll help you. He's not going to bite your hand off!"

The two boys cautiously walked forward following Beth's lead.

"See I don't allow people to feed the animals and I rarely ever give them hand treats so none of these animals' mistake fingers for treats and accidentally bite someone. So really boys, trust me, they are not going to bite you."

I could tell, and so could Beth, that the two youngsters needed more. So Beth continued with the education.

"Now, when you pet a horse you should walk up to their shoulder, not their head, and then give them a pat on the shoulder like this." As she demonstrates this move the two boys stand in amazement. I'm not sure what was so amazing, but they were certainly impressed. The demonstration must have boosted their confidence because they sheepishly stepped toward me and gave me a light pat on my shoulder and then quickly jumped back. Now here is where my professionalism comes in. Any other horse would have been startled by this very sudden movement. But both Molly (I taught her everything she knows) and I just stood very still. Besides, if just touching me is this frightening, I can only imagine their reaction if I were to sneeze right now.

"His hair is soft", one of the boys said.

"Of course it is. Jett gets a bath in the morning before he comes to places like this along with all the other animals. Jett also gets groomed before he is ridden.

I knew this was coming. "You ride him?"

Well, not as much as he used to be ridden but I still use him sometimes for riding lessons," Beth replies.

Now she has given them more information than they can process. "Can I pet her?" one asked pointing to Molly. Just using the tip of his fingers he lightly touched Molly. "She is kinda shaggy looking and she has really big ears. Can we pet the other animals?" "Sure, go ahead, just ask someone over there to help you. You might have to wait in line."

Just before those two boys turned to leave, I looked right into their eyes and saw something. I realized that I had probably touched their lives, maybe for just a brief moment, but I had made an impression. Then I looked at Beth and really saw that we had not made as much of an impression in their lives as they had in ours.

The Cast

We go many places as a petting farm, places like festivals and birthday parties, but of all the places we travel to, the ones I enjoy the most are the schools. The atmosphere at festivals and carnival-like events is sometimes very chaotic. Regardless of how many signs Beth puts up or how many times she says "Don't walk up behind the horse and donkey, they like to see who is petting them," people walk up behind us anyway. I get quite amused when I'm resting my back leg. People run up behind me, seeing my one leg resting and they will stop dead in their tracks swearing, at the top of their lungs that I am going to kick them.

When the traveling petting farm goes to schools or nursing homes Beth brings the animals out one at a time and gives a brief description about them, generally starting with the smallest to the largest. This order of presentation in no way reflects importance. I am, of course the largest and in my opinion the most important but

I am the last to be introduced to the crowd of onlookers. The smallest animals are the baby ducks, so they are first.

As she holds up a baby duck, one can hear all kinds of oohs and ahhs from both the children and the adults that are sitting in the grass beside the truck and trailer. "Who knows what this little guy is?" she says with a smile. Okay, like that's a hard question. Lots of hands are raised, but of course there is always one kid who feels they do not need to wait to be called on and yells at the top of his lungs "A DUCK!!'"

"Sure is, but this is a baby duck. My son and daughter helped me hatch these ducks out in our house. We collect the eggs from around my pond before anything gets them and then put the eggs in an incubator. We have to turn the eggs twice a day and spray water on them and then, after about 30 days, they hatch."

"Where is their mommy?" a little girl politely asks seeming a little worried about the fact that these cute things might not have a mom.

"I'm their mommy" Beth reassured her. "They only need their moms for warmth and protection, so that is why I keep them under a heat lamp in my house where they are warm and safe until they are big enough to be able to crawl out of the pond where all the other ducks live. Because what do ducks like to do?"

"SWIM!!!" I think every kid yelled this answer out at the same time. Again she keeps coming with the hard questions. Come on Beth, challenge these children.

"Okay what's this?" she asks touching the little duck's bill. "A beak!" the little know-it-all yells without waiting to be called upon. However, Beth has stumped them, unbelievable, with an easy one. "Nope it's called a bill on a duck," she said looking somewhat pleased that she has stumped them so easily. On she goes talking about webbed feet and other boring duck facts until finally she gives everyone a chance to pet the little thing reminding them to just use one finger because it is so little. I'd say maybe half the kids followed directions correctly.

Personally the ducks do not annoy me or any of the other horses back home on the farm. Occasionally we can hear the adult ducks all laugh, playing what sounds like a poker game down on the pond. Sometimes while Beth is in the riding arena teaching a lesson, they do a fly-by, but most of the horses are use to it.

Andy Goose, however, does get on my nerves sometimes because she is so loud. She is like the matriarch on the farm. Beth is a firm believer in making sure that every animal enjoys traveling and Andy was one that didn't. I don't speak fluent goose, but apparently Beth does. Andy told her she was not happy being put in a kennel, loaded in the horse trailer and then looked at all day. So she didn't have to travel anymore. Andy showed Beth her appreciation by being a very good watch goose. Every time a car came in the driveway that she was not familiar with, she would honk. She loved Beth very much. Sometimes she would sit on her lap while she taught a lesson or follow her around the riding arena while Beth walked and taught and rubbed up against her legs. Beth could even call Andy up from the pond to the front porch of the house and Andy would waddle towards her squawking the whole time, finally crawling into Beth's lap.

It has come to this horse's attention that with children, a certain comfort zone comes with something familiar. So the next animal presented to the children is the Basset Hound named Butter. Butter is a very good girl; if she were human she would be someone's grandmother. Because most everyone either has a dog or been around one, Butter is a good warm-up animal. After Beth reminds the kids to never pet a strange dog, she and Butter do a drive-by petting where even the adults participate. Another cuddly type animal is Gene, the Angora rabbit. Now this guy is truly my kind of animal to share the farm. He makes no noise. He hardly eats a thing; basically speaking, Gene keeps a very low profile. He thinks he's popular because he is allowed to be loose while everyone touches and feels his wool. I hate to break it to him but I'm the most popular.

Next in line, following along according to size, would be the chickens. Now I have to say, these creatures have not been, what a horse of my stature would call, a good addition to the farm. But Beth feels they are a necessary animal to have with the petting farm. It is this horse's opinion that they are dirty, loud, and downright disgusting. But as much as I hate to admit it, Beth is in charge, so I suppose they stay. I still can't believe that little hen, Betty, just sits on the palm of Beth's hand while she walks around letting everyone pet her. Even Red, the rooster, tries to impress everyone by occasionally crowing to the delight of some and terror of others. I think those chickens are show-offs, even more so then the pygmy goats.

Now, when one thinks rowdy, one must be thinking about the goats. The day that Jerry and Judy arrived on the farm was the day all life on the farm changed and would never be the same again. They care about only one thing and one thing only-what's there to eat! When they arrived on the farm, after being purchased from one of Beth's students' (I'm not quite sure of the students' motive behind this sale), the farm was on lockdown. These goats are escape artists and they get into everything, even my feed. So to reduce these incidents as much as possible, Beth had to lock the feed room. She even put bells on their collars around their necks so she could at least hear them while they were eating her flowers. These goats with their bell gave every horse on the farm a headache.

When Judy and Jerry are brought out of the kennel for the school children to see-well let's put it this way-they do not stand still. They drag whoever is attempting to hold them right towards food. Now Molly and I both watch this escapade each time and, as of yet, cannot figure out what they are trying to eat or, better yet, why? As Beth explains to the group of school children that a goat will eat anything, even something poisonous that could possible kill them or make them sick, I think why for heavens sake does she stop them from enjoying themselves? Molly and I are both in agreement; let them eat anything-please. I will admit that Judy and Jerry do produce lots of laughter, especially when they try to eat shoelaces. So I will give them credit where credit is due.

"Would you all like to meet my pot-bellied pig?" The group of children can hardly contain themselves now. The teachers and parent volunteers have asked them to sit still, but the thought of a pink pig coming out of the kennel into their safe little area on the grass is too much for some of them. I don't see why they are so excited; it's not my turn to be introduced yet. Oh well, let Julie have the spotlight for now. Soon it will be horse and donkey time.

The children watched in awe as Beth opened the door and coaxed Julie out of the kennel with a dog biscuit in her hand. "Normally I don't like to feed hand treats, but this is the only way I can convince Julie to do anything." No wonder she is an overweight pot-bellied pig. "I can get her to sit while everyone walks up slowly and gives her a scratch." Beth held the biscuit right in front of Julie's snout and all the children were able to get a turn. While every one was petting Julie, Beth explained how clean pigs are and how the term "sweating like a pig" is very incorrect. "Pigs aren't able to sweat. So when they get hot they cool themselves down by lying in a mud puddle." That educational little tidbit brought lots of comments.

"Now boys and girls, everyone has to sit down while I bring out the next two animals. I have to bring them out together because my sheep, Lilly, is blind and she has to follow the sound Tyler's bell." A hush came over the now captivated group. Personally, I think Lilly is faking the whole thing to get lots of sympathy. Beth and her daughter bring them out together positioning them in such a way that no on will get stepped on or kicked. Then she starts with all the sheep facts: wool, split hooves, blah, blah, blah. Then it's Holstein calf facts: Holsteins are black and white, where milk comes from, how chewing cud is like chewing gum. But sometimes these facts are too much for some groups.

Finally it is my turn. Molly and I are untied and led in the front of the group.

"This is my best friend, Jett. Jett has been my partner for many years. He is a registered Appaloosa gelding, meaning neutered male horse." She continues with other very interesting and important horse facts. "And this is his friend Molly the donkey. She has very large ears. Whose ears do you think are bigger-Molly's ears or Butter's ears?" This question from Beth brought on a lengthy discussion which finally concluded the program.

After the formal introduction to the animals, every child is invited to come up and pet the animals again and is allowed to go into the kennels with the animals. This is their opportunity to pet their personal favorite animal, which I knew, of course, everyone would flock to me. Some did come up and pet me again and some were petting other animals. I notice some special needs children that were in wheel chairs and on crutches. This was my specialty because I have done this at the nursing homes, where I have to walk up to the wheelchairs, get real close and then lower my head so I can be pet. I also know to be still while a wheelchair is being pushed practically under me.

I was feeling very proud of myself when I noticed Lilly. Lilly was not near Tyler where I know she feels the most comfortable. She was near a little girl who was getting some assistance reaching out with one hand to feel Lilly's wool. I heard one of the teachers talking to the girl describing the things she was feeling because she was blind just like Lilly. It was at this moment I realized that I was no more important to this petting farm than any other animal. I was just a piece of the puzzle, a big important piece, but just one piece.

Solo Appearances

All of us animals did not always travel together. Molly would sometimes do solo appearances at churches. It seemed that most of the churches that wanted Molly were located in the city.

Palm Sunday seemed to be the popular day for hiring Molly for her expertise in looking and acting biblical. However, it never seemed to fail that rain was generally part of the day's adventure when Molly would go to church in the city.

The things Molly would tell me when she returned to the farm were very interesting. She and I both agree that some of the things people do when they are around animals will never cease to amaze us. Her favorite is the waving of the palms. Palm waving was not too traumatizing until people did it behind Molly's back. And better yet, they think that the whole palm waving thing seems more realistic if the palms actually touch her on her rump. Do they not see that donkey's eyes (and horses' for that matter) are on the side of their heads? This feature enables us to see things to the side of us, but not directly in front of us, and most certainly not behind us. Therefore, waving and touching Molly with palms where she can't see what people are doing is a bit traumatic, but she was able to tolerate.

Rain did not stop Molly's visits to the city churches. Neither did the fact that most animals find it very difficult to walk up human steps. But when it means that walking up steps leads to being able to stand in the only dry place in the city, Molly walked up the steps without any problems. The rain also proposed another problem for Molly. Molly has confided in me that she feels her eyesight is fading and this became evident to Beth one rainy Palm Sunday in the city. When rain falls on concrete and blacktop it tends to look like ice. And any donkey knows ice is bad news if they have to walk on it. Beth can be pretty convincing most of the time, but donkeys can be very stubborn. And on that rainy day, Beth could not convince Molly to keep her hooves on the sidewalk. So the Palm Sunday parade route took several detours off the sidewalk that rainy day. Wherever Molly walked, the parade of church goers followed, enjoying themselves immensely.

Beth, her daughter, and a helper loaded Molly into the trailer to drive to the next church in the city. This is what Beth calls a double-booking. This particular church was ever farther into the world of concrete and blacktop. What Molly described to me next, this horse couldn't believe. This church had their very own jazz band. Everyone sang and danced and waved palms while Beth led Molly once again in a parade. Molly was not real impressed that apparently every child who attended the church wanted to have a turn playing "Jesus" and therefore be able to ride Molly, regardless of their size.

If concentrating on the parade route and carrying "Jesus" was not enough, right behind Molly everyone was singing, "Ride on little 'Jesus'. Ride on" waving palms while the jazz band played. When Molly was at the end of the parade (which so happened to be the front of the church), the Pastor asked if they could just walk right into the church! Hardly in a position to refuse, Molly and Beth walked right up the steps and into the church and up to the front where it was even more crowded with people. There they stood while some more songs were sung and then they turned around and walked out of the church.

Nativity scenes were another popular request for the petting farm which I for some reason, did not have a role. This job called for the sheep, the calf, the goats and camels. There weren't any camels available, so this enabled Beth to have the excuse to purchase a llama. Better yet, llamas need company of their own species so two llamas had to be purchased, enter JP and Major.

I understand from speaking with all the other animals after a nativity scene, the only real problem with this particular gig was the fact that these jobs were at night when it was very cold and, once again, in the city. This meant a long drive and occasionally wrong turns on Beth's part.

Nativity scenes were easy for most of the animals. All they had to do was to be lead or held while they ate hay. Molly had the work, once again, of providing every child involved in the nativity scene production the opportunity of playing "Mary", even the rather large ones. Now Molly is generally very tolerant, but at this one particular nativity scene she was not! It was cold that night and her back was stiff and the street was very busy and all this distracted her. "Mary" was just too large and she wasn't going to carry "Big Mary" to any stable and Molly tried to buck her off! Beth quickly pulled the "Big Mary" off before anyone really noticed.

I tried telling Molly, later that evening when every one returned to the farm and I heard of the events, that was no excuse for bad behavior.

During a Nativity scene every animal had to be held individually and held tightly because most of the nativity scenes were along busy roads. Molly said it was very embarrassing when the goats tried to eat the baby "Jesus" doll. Quickly the good goat handlers grabbed "Jesus" out of Jerry's mouth and persuaded him to eat the hay instead while the nativity songs were sung. I consoled Molly and told her not to be too embarrassed. We all know about the goat's eating disorder of "eat anything and everything".

Another solo job for the smaller petting farm animals was one at what I'm guessing, from what Betty the hen described, was an airport. Now I'm not sure how reliable all her facts are because of her poor eyesight, they should make eye glasses for chickens.

Betty explained to me that she and Gene, a couple of ducks, Tyler and Lilly all were loaded on the trailer complete with red bows tied to them or their cages on a very cold Saturday. The truck and trailer were driven out onto what seemed to be like a very, very big parking lot with very large and loud metal birdlike machines. I'm assuming she must have seen some airplanes on an airport runway. Betty said she saw some men with things covering their ears and waving to the big metal birds. These men then helped Beth and her helpers unload the animals in cages. Betty, Gene, and the ducks were put on a moving ladder that was very steep and led into a hallway. They were then carried to a lobby. Betty said it was very warm inside, but she was a little bit scared. She saw hundred of people walking around fast and carrying boxes with handles.

I asked Tyler and Lilly how they got into the building because they were too big and weren't able to use the moving platform ladder. Tyler, complete with bell around his neck, was led into a very small room with one of those men. And when the door closed, they said it felt like the floor moved straight up. When the sliding doors opened, Tyler and Lilly were on a different floor. Tyler said they were led through lots of people who all seemed to be quite amazed at seeing a calf and a sheep in the building, not to mention being outfitted with bells and red bows. Tyler also said that he and Lilly were scared.

Once they were settled in with the rest of the animals by a large door, Christmas music started to play. After a while the large door opened and a group of children came walking through the doors. Betty said she had never seen such happy children in all her petting farm days. These children smiled so much and petted the animal so nicely that all the animals were no longer scared. The children did a great job of comforting them.

Betty said most of these happy children did not have any hair and their skin was very pale. She heard something about dreams and wishes and realized she and the other animals were requested by these amazingly happy children and then understood that these children were very sick. Betty then felt a little bit silly about being scared around such brave children.

I told her "job well done".

On the Road

Beth was a fanatic about the well being of all of her animals. It was not only important to her that we were all happy and comfortable but she wanted to be sure anybody visiting the petting farm could tell that all the animals were all well cared for.

This became very evident at one festival when Beth overheard some lady make the comment while looking at the goats, "Poor animals, having to be here all day and let all these people pet them." Bodyguard Beth was at that lady's side in an instant with the following reply: "If all the children in the world were taken care of as well as these animals, what a wonderful world it would be. Maam, these animals are like children to me. They are fed good quality hay and grain; they all have plenty of cool, fresh water, not to mention routine grooming and baths. They sleep on clean bedding and get regular visits by the veterinarian. The horse even has his own dentist. They are able to travel and get all this attention. They are exercised and loved. Now can you tell me why you think they should be considered 'Poor animals'???" The woman's face turned red as she turned and walked quickly away.

In order for all of us to be comfortable at a job, it required a lot of work. This usually means hours of work day before an event. The original pens for the first two jobs Beth's husband made of plywood, but they were just too heavy to manage. So chain link kennels were used. These were then rigged up to be transported on the side of the horse trailer. This enabled there to be more room for other things in the bed of the truck. The bed of the truck hauled the pitch forks, rakes, a broom and the manure basket. In the event of extreme sun and heat, Beth even has two tents in the back of the truck to shade the animals. Chairs for the helpers and a cooler with food and drink were also packed.

The trailer was packed with grain for each animal. There was rabbit food for the rabbit, calf food for the calf, duck food for the ducks, chicken food for the chickens, sheep food for the sheep, some sort of pig food and of course, something to keep the goats happy. Hay was packed for Molly, me and a little for everyone else. We also had to have bedding in the event the job was on black top. Water was brought from the farm in a big barrel because some of the places we went, the water had chlorine in it and then we would not drink like we should. Bringing water from the farm enable us to drink familiar-tasting water. Grooming tools were packed along with fly sprays, medicines (both human and animal), and other first aid equipment. Posters and brochures about the animals, along with decorations and even a farm flag were displayed. She even went as far as color coordinating all the buckets, I'm told because horses are color blind.

These are the supplies needed for a one-day job.

When it came time to load all the animals, I was the last to be loaded so I stood in my stall and watched in awe how Beth strategically loaded animals. First it was Gene in at his kennel, and then it was the chickens that were usually caught at night while they were roosting. Next were the ducks who were now loose on the farm and meant that Beth and her helpers had to run around catching them the morning before we left the farm. Next to last to be put in a kennel were Judy and Jerry. All of the animals that are in kennels were put in the gooseneck part of the trailer, which is the part that actually is hooked in the bed of the truck, not behind the truck.

Now it is time to load the larger livestock. First is Tyler, with that loud bell, and Lilly follows him. Lilly walks right on the trailer which is why I think she is faking the whole blind thing. Just because she fell into a big hole one day and sometimes bumps into things now and then, Beth thinks she is blind. Well, she was able to step into the trailer today just fine. Then all the help had to lift Julie in her kennel onto the trailer. Boy did their faces get red as they lifted that kennel.

Molly and I are the last to be loaded. I do love my friend, Molly, dearly. But she has one bad habit-she likes to drag people around sometimes. I have spoken to her about this rather-rude behavior, but she still does it occasionally, especially to new help when they try to load her on the trailer. I, of course, am the perfect horse. No one even has to lead me on the trailer. Just throw the lead over my neck and say "Get on Jett" and I get on the trailer perfectly.

Butter gets to ride up in the front with Beth, her daughter, her sister-in-law and another teenage student, all of whom are helping today. We are taking along with us on this job a pygmy goat named Elizabeth. Elizabeth is, believe it or not, riding up front with them because she has a cast on her leg. It seems that Elizabeth got in a field with some horses on the farm and one of them kicked her in the leg. X-rays showed a broken leg that needed a cast. I think she did it just for attention and to be able to ride up in the front of the truck. Finally all the animals are loaded and out the driveway we go.

On the road again very early in the morning, I have my usual spot by the window. There was a cool breeze coming in the window. I knew it was going to be one of those days that would get real hot later. I have a good view from my window. Everyone in the trailer was being somewhat quite and everything was very peaceful until I heard the truck make some very funny sounds.

We weren't driving very long when the truck pulled off to the side of the road. I heard something about running out of gas because the gas gauge was broken on the truck All of them were debating who was going to have to walk to the nearest gas station. As per usual, we were in a hurry and whoever had to walk had to do it quickly.

By now traffic was picking up on the dual lane highway and I could see lots of cars driving past the trailer. It was decided that the sister-in-law and the teenage would try to get gas or help. Off they ran down the highway. A great deal of time went by and I could sense Beth's worry. I knew she was worried about getting to the job on time and the welfare of her helpers.

More time went past and then I heard a horn and lots of yelling and screaming. Looking out my window, I caught a glimpse of the sister-in-law and teenager waving to us from the back of a pick-up-truck, traveling on the highway at what seemed like a high rate of speed and going in the opposite direction.

"Hey Beth, we got gas!! We'll be there as soon as we turn around!" they yelled to Beth who was standing beside her trailer in disbelief at the speed the truck was traveling and the fact that it was on the opposite side of the highway! Sure enough, in a few seconds the truck appeared behind the trailer and out jumped Beth's helpers safe and sound with a gas can full of gas and then the pick-up-truck sped away.

"Thank you!!!" she said a bit relieved "Whose was that guy?"

"We have no idea. He just said he would help us out!!" Boy, were they brave or stupid? I'm not sure which, but we were on the road again.

We once again started down the now-busy highway when I heard a very loud noise. We pulled off the highway again and the sister-in-law got out of the truck and yelled "Beth, your tent blew out of the truck and is now scattered in pieces all along the highway. Don't worry, I'll run and gather it up off of the road." Was there no end to this woman's bravery and dedication?

Finally, we arrived at the festival which happened to be in the middle of a closed off street. It was very hot on the blacktop and many people were there to see the farm animals.

Setting up was a time consuming job. Everything had to be in order before any of the animals could be taken off the trailer. And more often than not, we had an audience. I could always hear fifty questions from the curious children even before one animal was unloaded. Lots of times Beth would have to ask them to come back later, but that never worked. They stayed and watched the animals being unloaded asking all about the animals while Beth and her helpers were very busy.

Just as I expected it was very hot and the sun was very bright. Beth was able to duct tape the tent together enough to provide some relief from the sun. It was hot, so the ice bottles that were brought for Gene provided him with some relief and Julie would get water thrown on her to keep her cool. The rest of us really do fine in the heat.

And for the sister-in-law, well she got some new sandals so she could sunbathe and get some sun on her feet while sitting on the hot blacktop with the animals. This kept the help happy and comfortable, too.

Our Home

The farm where I live is primarily a horse farm. Beth and her husband built it themselves. It is not very big but all the animals that live here, whether it is long-term or short-term, like it. The farm was named after Beth's first pony; I think it should have been named after me.

We have several pastures and paddocks for all the horses. There is a stream in two of the pastures. The ducks have a pond and the llamas share a field with the goats and the sheep. The pig gets to roam around and eats all the food that gets spilled. It is a peaceful co-existence on the farm- every animal gets along with every animal.

Every time I turned around there was a different animal living on the farm. The most exotic was the baby emu named Julian. Beth purchased him when he was little and she was in hopes that he would imprint on her like Andy Goose. She worked very hard with that emu, going as far as training him to run in a harness with her husband. Julian was even permitted to run loose and went sled riding with the family. Julian did go on several jobs with us, but he was just too intimidating for the children to pet. He developed a dangerous habit of kicking and became increasingly difficult to handle as he grew bigger. He also had a taste for earrings, especially the ones in Beth's ears. Unfortunately, Julian had to find a new home and all the horses on the farm were very happy about his leaving. That emu was just too weird; the term birdbrain described him well. The farm and the petting farm had to be a group effort and the emu just didn't fit in.

The horse farm also turned into some sort of a sheep breeding operation. Beth and one of her good friends decided to get into the lambing business. I'm surprised they stuck with it after the initial tragedy. Lilly died trying to give birth to twin lambs. Death is a part of life even in the animal world and Beth got some new ewes and tried the lambing thing again. This time she was even more determined not to lose any ewes or lambs. Her friend had a nursing background which came in handy during lambing season. I heard that they even took lambs into the house to live by the warm woodstove and be fed with a tube and then a bottle to ensure their survival.

One winter, lambing season had been extremely busy and the last ewe to lamb gave birth to triplets. All of the students fell in love with one of the triplets that was very weak and almost died. Beth was just too busy for any more lambs in the house so a student took her home and nursed her back to life. She would bring the lamb to the farm for "Beth's daycare" while she went to school, picking up the tiny thing when school was finished. Needless to say the lamb became a favorite and took over Lilly's role in the petting farm. Because of her small size, her name was Ounce. Ounce has grown up and even produced offspring of her own, Pint and Quart, but all she has to do now is travel with the petting farm.

I knew from the beginning that Julie was going to develop weight problems because of her poor eating habits. I spoke with her about it, she did not listen and she became overweight. She was not so overweight that it was a serious health issue, but overweight enough that she could not be lifted into the kennel in the trailer. Julie had been such a good pig- doing sit-stay tricks for children and even tolerating Judy and Jerry jumping on her back like a jungle gym. But I could understand Beth's point that she was just too heavy to lift. So Buck, the new pot-bellied pig, entered the petting farm. Beth was able to find Julie a good home with a student who was a very good friend. This enabled Beth to provide Buck with a home because the person he lived with (in someone's house just like Julie did) needed to find him a home. Buck seems the same as Julie, all he cares about is food and finding a comfortable place to sleep in the barn. He was smaller and easier to lift. The helpers' faces didn't seem to get quite as red loading him onto the trailer.

I'm not sure whose bright idea it was, but I heard mention that the petting farm was going to participate in the local fireman's' annual parade. This sound like a little more work than standing tied to the horse trailer. And what I heard next upset me even more. Apparently, all the animals were going to be in this parade. However, the trailer was not large enough to transport everyone. So because it was considered close enough to walk to the start, guess who got nominated to be led to the town for the parade? None other than Molly and myself. Excuse me, but what happened to seniority? I guess those llamas get our spot on the trailer and we have to walk to town, then in the parade, and back home. Lucky us!

Molly and I started our journey an hour before the rest of the clan. Generally I can talk Molly into or out of almost anything, but on that summer evening she wasn't about to listen to my advice or the persuading of Beth's friend that was leading her into town for the parade. On our journey into town there was a bridge that we needed to cross. Molly took one look at it, planted her hooves and did not move for an hour! After awhile, Beth's friend took off her sweat shirt and blindfolded Molly's eyes. That didn't work either. It wasn't until she had turned Molly around in circles several times and backed her across the bridge that we could finally continue our journey to the parade. Molly should have listened to me. It would have been a lot less work and aggravation for all of us.

We made it to the parade just in time to start walking while all the other animals that were in their kennels got to ride in the back of a horse-drawn wagon. The whole crew was all there: Butter, Judy, Jerry, Elizabeth (her cast was off), Ounce, Norman the new calf, Major, JP, Gene, Red the rooster, Betty, Sweet Pea and Sunshine the ducks, and Buck. Beth had all kinds of help leading and watching these animals. I had a laugh while her son and daughter lead the goats; people were calling the goats dogs! The children loved the animals walking over during the parade route for them to pet. And when Molly heard someone yell "Look at the beautiful donkey!" she was glad she had been in the parade and finally had walked across the bridge. She liked to be noticed. Being recognized and gaining a little confidence sure did a lot for her. Molly walked right over the bridge to go back home.

The Fair

The trailer was being loaded with every possible supply one hot day in July. In fact it seemed that Beth was making several trips to somewhere with all out petting farm gear. This truly had me puzzled; all these trips with what seemed like triple the normal amount of supplies. We all had the usual baths and it seemed that we all were obviously going somewhere. Usually it is either the llamas or Molly and me taken to a job, never all of us because we all can't fit into the same trailer. This time the llamas were loaded on the trailer and left. Beth came back without them and then loaded Molly and I, along with the rest of the menagerie, and off we went. This had me very concerned.

It was a short drive to our destination. As Molly and I were unloaded I knew the moment my hooves hit the blacktop where I was. I was at the 4-H County Fair! I knew this place because Beth and I had competed here years ago when we both were younger. Not much had changed.

There were still the same rustic looking buildings that housed 4-Her's animals and the same big, red building that displayed 4-Her's baking, art and much more. The food stands were the same, but a little older looking. The road that led right down the middle of all these building was worn. There were trailers everywhere unloading 4-Her's cattle, sheep, pigs, and cars unloading everything from ducks to rabbits to crafts. It was certainly busy and I could sense the excitement in the air.

Molly and I were led under a big tent and that is where I saw the llamas. It was at this point that I realized we were the petting farm at the 4-H fair. The two chain link kennels were under the tent along with two other larger kennels. There was even a feed room. At each end of the tent were two huge fans that were already blowing the air around making it much cooler under the tent than outside. I saw all kinds of flowers and decorations. At one end under the tent were two small metal rocking horses that had saddles on them, I guess children sat on them. Better they sit on those metal horses than on me! In the middle of the tent there was a table where coloring books were displayed and on some of the tent post there were hand wash things for people to wash their hands. I could sense from the way Beth was running around, that this was a pretty important job, so I told everyone to be on their best behavior. I also had the feeling that we all would be living here for at least several days, judging by the amount of hay and food I saw in the feed room.

Day one started out like most jobs did anywhere else. People were standing waiting to come into the tent to visit us. Beth always tried to talk to as many people as possible, trying to educate those that were unfamiliar with farming, farm animals and farm life. The volunteers helping would answer as many questions as they could and, of course, helping everyone pet the animals; "Hands-on experience" was what I heard Beth tell a lot of people. She would take me out of my stall and lead me on the blacktop road in front of the tent so everyone could see me better. Sometimes she would demonstrate how to tell a horse's age by looking at their teeth. I didn't mind her opening my mouth and showing everyone that I was getting old although some kids thought my teeth looked disgusting. Well, maybe that will make you brush your teeth, kids. Even Ounce was brought out in front of the tent when she had a halter on and let everyone feel her wool. When wheel chairs carrying children and adults could not get into the tent, animals were brought out to them.

Beth had so much help during fair week, but it was before the fair that one particular person was very important to the success of the petting farm. He was my farrier (the man who trims our hooves). Whenever Beth needed to find a particular animal to complete the petting farm she would call on him. When JP died, she needed another llama quickly to be a companion to Major. So she called on her farrier and he found her a baby llama which Beth named Doolittle. Always smiling and never in a bad mood, he knew a lot about animals and horses. We have other farriers on the farm that are very good at trimming our hooves and putting on shoes, but this man has so much knowledge about all types of farm animals. He even had a special trick to make Molly stand still while her hooves are trimmed. This is not always an easy task. To this day Molly still stands still for our farrier.

The help at the fair was great and only made a few mistakes. One time someone decided to tie Elizabeth to a chair that they were sitting on and when they got up, Elizabeth went off running through the crowd of people with the chair flying behind her! Jerry and Judy also added a little stress to Beth's life by sometimes running right out the gate as a helper opened it for children to enter. I have spoken with them several times about this obnoxious thing they do but they say they do it to make sure the helpers are paying attention.

The fair was open rain or shine. The admission price was free and there were all kinds of entertainment. Various local bands played on the stage and in the building beside the petting farm tent. The music was loud, but we all got used to it and we were sometimes even able to sleep through the loud entertainment. The only thing that reduced the size of the crowd was a summer thunderstorm. Sometimes the storms were so severe that our tent would feel like it would almost blow down and fair officials would run in and help with storm management. One time the tent was touching my ears.

The amount of people visiting was almost overwhelming for us, Beth, and her helpers. All kinds of people visited-the kind that knew it all and the kind that were generally interested in hearing about us. Some people were clean freaks using the hand wash stuff after petting each animal. My favorite was the father who saw the hand wash stuff and told his children it was there for them to wash their hands before they touch the animals, like it meant that their hands were dirty and we were clean. I liked that father.

Now Beth is not a very big lady. In fact, she is kind of short. But she is very brave, especially when it comes to our defense. She had to time, and time again, tell people not to worry about the llamas spitting. They rarely spit and as long as they are not aggravated, they will not spit at all. Because of the popularity of the petting farm, it was always crowded. So all Beth could really do some evenings was just stand in a corner and keep an eagle eye on things. One evening (I saw the whole thing happen), Beth saw two rather large older men talking and staring at Major and Doolittle. Then, for no apparent reason, one of the men spit on poor Doolittle! Beth jumped down immediately from her spot in the tent and ran to Doolittle's rescue.

"Excuse me Sir, why did you spit on my llama?" she asked him looking way up because he was about three times her size.

"I didn't spit on your llama," he looked down on her, trying to intimidate her with his size.

"Yes, you did. I can see your spit on his neck. That was mean and you are going to have to leave," she ordered him seemingly like she was now bigger than he was. The man looked a little smaller to me after Beth said that and turned and walked out of the tent grumbling. We never saw that man or his friend again.

The other people that amaze me are the people that think they know the animals better than Beth. Several years ago, Judy had a kid (baby goat) and was named Barbara. Barbara was a cute little white goat just like Judy. After she was about 6 months old, she started to grow, what looked like, a knot on the side of her neck. This worried Beth because it kept getting bigger, Barbara was taken to the veterinarian's office and had an x-ray taken. The results were unbelievable. Barbara's neck was broken! The fact that this cute little goat was still alive was a miracle. Barbara could eat and drink fine, run fine, and in fact, other than her head looking like it was on crooked, she was fine. The only thing she could not do was scratch herself on the right side of her back. Barbara was part of the petting farm that year at the fair. She loved having children scratch her, but somebody must have been offended by her looks and thought it was cruel to have her in the kennel with the other goats for children to pet.

One afternoon while the petting farm was closed for a couple of hours, Beth went home to check on the horses. When she came back, she was stopped at the entrance gate of the fair. It seemed that someone thought it was cruel to have Barbara at the fair so they had called the Animal Police and the State Police! By the time Beth got to the petting farm tent all the excitement was over because Beth's sister-in-law was a good diplomat. She told the officers that the animals had all their vaccinations, health papers, and everything else that they might have needed. Barbara never came to the fair again but enjoys her life thinking she is in charge of things at the farm and eating any important notes left out in the barn. Typical goat, eating anything and everything.

Beth continued to do the petting farm at the fair. It has almost become a yearly reunion. I would get to see some of my past pupils that I have taught to ride. Some I haven't seen for years. Everyone commented on how great I look, like I don't already know this. We even have people come to the fair actually looking for us to revisit.

The whole fairgrounds were actually on a hill therefore it made it difficult to push people in wheelchairs back up the stony hill after going down to see the livestock in the barns. One afternoon there was an older lady struggling to push an elderly lady in a wheelchair up the hill. They both were smiling regardless of their difficulty and the heat. They stopped in front of the petting farm tent so the animals could visit with this cheerful mother and daughter. For years the pair made it an annual visit to the petting farm remembering all the animals' names and recognizing new faces like the new llama, Doolittle. One year we saw the smiling face of the daughter, but not the wheelchair with the mother. The daughter said her mom had passed away, but she herself would not miss the fair and her opportunity to visit with the petting farm animals. I can only imagine how much that daughter misses her mother. I know sometimes I miss Andy Goose and her loud honk, who is no longer with us. Maybe our farrier will find a new baby goose to add to our petting farm family.

Change in the petting farm's roster is difficult sometimes. Change in everyday life is difficult, but sometimes change happens for the best. Change can mean progress. I understand that the buildings at the fair are all being torn down. The knoll that was difficult to push wheelchairs up is gone. There is a new, bigger building for the whole fair and the petting farm. Now even a thunderstorm can't keep crowds of people away that come to see me do my job. One thing I hope will never change is the desire for the young and young-at-heart to see and pet an animal like myself and all my partners, old and new, in the petting farm.

About the Author

Beth T. Stambaugh grew up on a livestock farm in Westminster, Maryland. At an early age, she developed a love for farm animals and a passion for horses.

Beth and Jett have been partners for 25 plus years and, with lots of help from friends and family, have done the petting farm for nearly 10 years.

While Beth continues to train horses and teach riding lessons, Jett is living the high life. He is enjoying his retirement on his farm with Beth and her family.